Easy Hymn Duets

For 1 Piano, 4 Hands
By Wesley Schaum

T0210379

Foreword

A great music educator once said, "Rhythm is caught, not taught." Duet playing provides valuable experience developing a sense of rhythm.

These duets are designed for two students at the same level – primo and secondo parts are of *equal difficulty*. Both parts are fun to learn because both players are given interesting accompaniments as well as melodies.

It is suggested that a student alternate parts, learning the primo part for one piece, the secondo part for the next, etc. This gives valuable sight-reading experience with both hands in treble clef and with both hands in bass clef.

Duet playing provides an excellent opportunity for *ear training*. Emphasis should be placed on *listening carefully* to both parts so that the melody can be heard clearly and the accompaniment subdued.

These hymn duets are ideal for recitals and for Sunday school use.

Index

EXCLUSIVELY DISTRIBUTED BY

7777 W. BLUEMOUND RD. P.O. BOX 13819 MILWAUKEE, WI 53213

© Copyright 1969 by Schaum Publications, Inc., Mequon, Wisconsin
International Copyright Secured • All Rights Reserved • Printed in U.S.A.

All Hail the Power of Jesus' Name

SECONDO

DIRECTIONS: One secret of good ensemble playing is to **PLAY THE ACCOMPANIMENT SOFTLY** so that the melody can be heard easily. In order to achieve this, **YOU MUST LISTEN CAREFULLY** as you play.

To help locate the melody, *words have been printed only where there is melody*. So, if your part has words — be sure to bring out the melody. If your part does *not* have words — play the accompaniment softly.

All Hail the Power of Jesus' Name

PRIMO

DIRECTIONS: One secret of good ensemble playing is to PLAY THE ACCOMPANIMENT SOFTLY so that the melody can be heard easily. In order to achieve this, YOU MUST LISTEN CAREFULLY as you play.

To help locate the melody, *words have been printed only where there is melody.* So, if your part has words — be sure to bring out the melody. If your part does *not* have words — play the accompaniment softly.

Blest Be the Tie That Binds

SECONDO

Blest Be the Tie That Binds

PRIMO

Stand Up, Stand Up for Jesus

SECONDO

Stand Up, Stand Up for Jesus

PRIMO

REMINDER: To help locate the melody, *words have been printed only where there is melody.* So, if your part has words — be sure to bring out the melody. If your part does *not* have words — play the accompaniment softly.

Jesus Wants Me for a Sunbeam

SECONDO

Jesus Wants Me for a Sunbeam

PRIMO

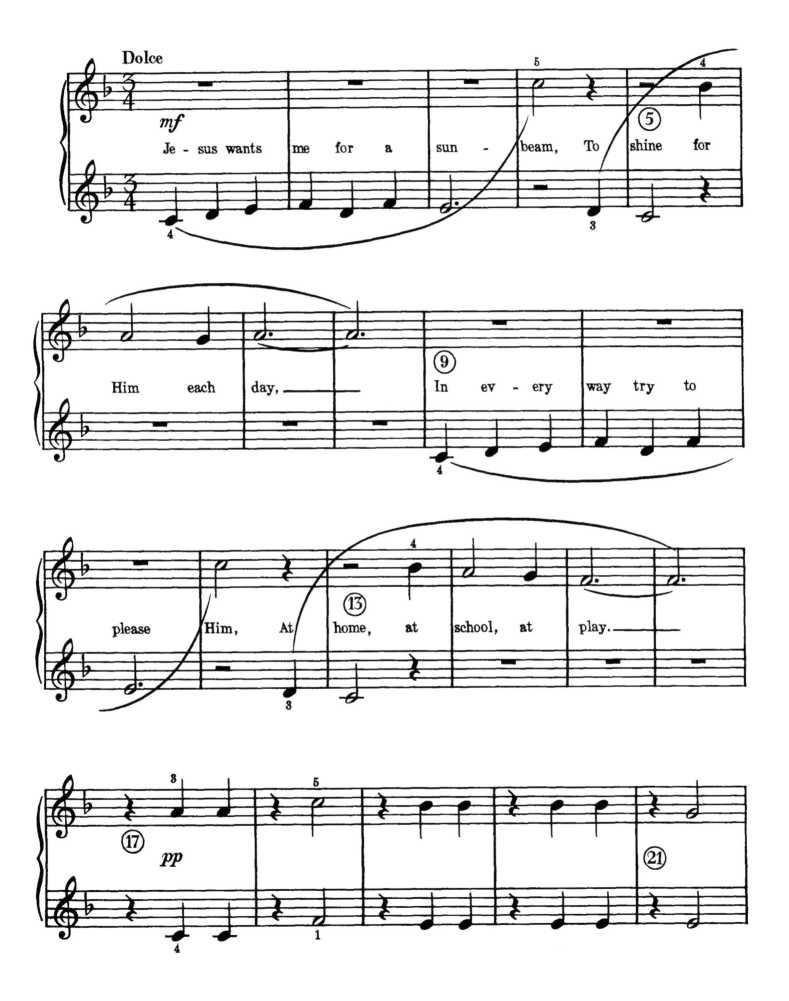

Jesus Wants Me for a Sunbeam - continued
SECONDO

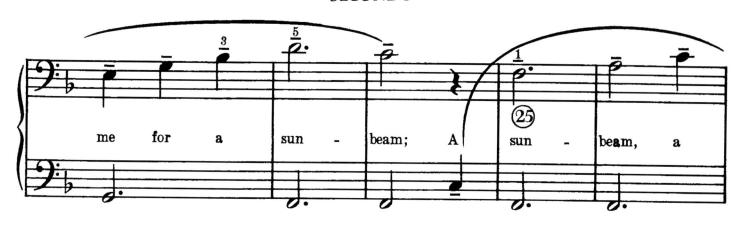

me for a sun - beam; A sun - beam, a

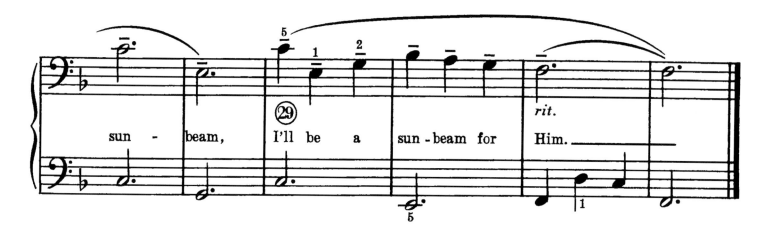

sun - beam, I'll be a sun - beam for Him.

Fling Out the Banner
SECONDO

Jesus Wants Me for a Sunbeam - continued
PRIMO

Fling Out the Banner
PRIMO

Fling | out the ban-ner! | let it float Sky- | ward and sea-ward | high and wide; The

sun that lights its | shin - ing folds, The | Cross on which the | Sav - iour died.

Come Thou Almighty King

SECONDO

Come Thou Almighty King

PRIMO

REMINDER: One secret of good duet playing is to PLAY THE ACCOMPANIMENT SOFTLY so that the melody can be heard easily. In order to achieve this, YOU MUST LISTEN CAREFULLY as you play.

Faith of Our Fathers

SECONDO

Faith of Our Fathers

PRIMO

Faith of Our Fathers - continued
SECONDO

Father Lead Me Day by Day

SECONDO

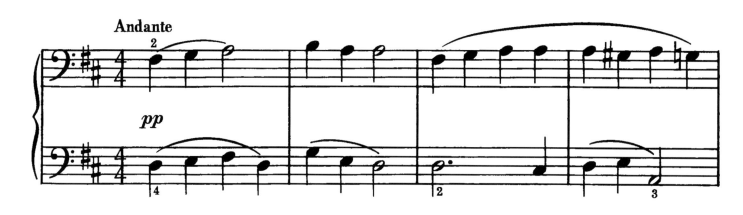

PRIMO

Father Lead Me Day by Day

PRIMO

Fa-ther lead me | day— by day, | Ev - er in Thine | own sweet way;

Teach me to be | pure and true; Show me | what— I | ought to do.

Holy, Holy, Holy

SECONDO

Early in the morn - ing our songs shall rise to Thee,

Per - fect in pow'r, in love and pur - i - ty.

Holy, Holy, Holy

PRIMO

Fairest Lord Jesus

SECONDO

Fairest Lord Jesus

PRIMO

God Be With You Till We Meet Again

SECONDO

God Be With You Till We Meet Again

PRIMO

God of Our Fathers

SECONDO

God of our fa - thers, whose al - might - y hand

Leads forth in beau - ty

God of Our Fathers

PRIMO

What a Friend We Have in Jesus

SECONDO

What a Friend We Have in Jesus

PRIMO

Onward Christian Soldiers

SECONDO

Onward Christian Soldiers

PRIMO

Onward Christian Soldiers - continued
SECONDO

Now the Day Is Over

SECONDO

Onward Christian Soldiers - continued
PRIMO

With the cross of Je - sus Go - ing on be - fore.

Now the Day Is Over
PRIMO

Now the day is o - ver, Night is draw-ing___ nigh,___

Sha - dows of the eve - ning Steal a - cross the sky.

Successful Schaum Sheet Music

This is a Partial List — Showing Level 1 through Level 2

☝ = 5 Finger Position   * = Big Notes   • = Original Form   ✓ = Chord Symbols

ACTION SOLOS

			LEVEL
55-10 *•	ABOMINABLE SNOWMAN (Left Hand Melody)	Durocher	2
52-07 *•	ASTRONAUT ADVENTURE (Left Hand Melody)	Schaum	1
52-25 *•	BUBBLE BLUES	Weston	1
55-20 *	POGO STICK CHOP (Based on "Chop Sticks")	Schaum	2
55-34 *•	RIGHT ON (Staccato)	Miller	2
55-26 •	WATER SLIDE (Staccato)	Payne	2

AMERICAN – PATRIOTIC SOLOS

55-14	AMERICA THE BEAUTIFUL	Ward	2
55-41	MARINES' HYMN	Traditional	2
55-08	WABASH CANNON BALL	Railroad Song	2

ANIMALS and BIRDS

52-16 *•	BUSY WOODPECKER ☝ (Staccato)	Cahn	1
52-29 •	BUZZY AND WUZZY (Two Kittens)	Maier	1
52-36 •	DINOSAUR LAND	Schaum	1
52-38 •	KANGAROO HOP ☝	Polk	1
52-24 *•	PERKY TURKEY	Weston	1
55-09 *•	POPPO the PORPOISE (Left Hand Melody)	Littlewood	2

BOOGIE

55-07 *•	COOL SCHOOL (Boogie Style)	Schaum	2
55-02 •	LITTLE DOG BOOGIE	Schaum	2

BOTH HANDS in TREBLE CLEF

52-27 •	JOYOUS BELLS ☝ (with Duet Accompaniment)	Cahn	1
55-44 •	MYSTICAL ETUDE (Staccato)	Cahn	2

CHRISTMAS

70-10 *	IT CAME UPON THE MIDNIGHT CLEAR	Traditional	1
81-01 *✓	IT'S BEGINNING TO LOOK LIKE CHRISTMAS		2
81-06	LITTLE DRUMMER BOY, The	Arr. Schaum	1
70-02	TWELVE DAYS of CHRISTMAS	All 12 Verses	1
70-01 *	WHAT CHILD IS THIS? ("Greensleeves")	Traditional	1

CIRCUS

55-39 •	CIRCUS PONIES	Leach	2

CLASSICS

52-09 *	Beethoven	SONG of JOY ("Ode To Joy" from 9th Symph.)	1
52-37	Grieg	In the HALL of the MOUNTAIN KING	1
52-12 ✓	Handel	HALLELUJAH CHORUS (Easy Edition)	1
55-30	Mozart	MOZART'S ROMANCE (from "A Little Night Music")	2
55-45	Pachelbel	PACHELBEL'S CANON (Easy Edition)	2
52-35	Rossini	WILLIAM TELL MARCH	1

COUNTRY/WESTERN

55-35	DAGGER DANCE ("Land of Sky Blue Waters")	Herbert	2
52-06 *•	PONY RIDE ☝	McCreary	1

DESCRIPTIVE MUSIC

52-39 •	ANCIENT PAGODA	Biel	1
52-17 *•	CHARM BRACELET	Cahn	1
55-46 •	COME BACK TO SORRENTO	deCurtis	2
55-47 •	DOMINOES	Cahn	2
52-32 *•	GLIDING ON THE WIND	Hampton	1
55-49 •	IN A FAR OFF TIME & PLACE	Revezoulis	2
52-40 •	JOLLY LEPRECHAUN	Revezoulis	1
55-51 •	PEACEFUL INTERLUDE	Holmes	2
55-37 •	PICTURE POSTCARD (w/Duet Accompaniment)	Cahn	2
52-14 *•	SLUMBER PARTY	Stecker	1
55-42 •	SUNSET SERENADE	Levin	2

DISSONANCE

55-32 •	ROBOT TALK (Staccato)	Cray	2
55-27 •	VIDEO GAME (Staccato)	Russell/Schaum	2

DUET (1 Piano, 4 Hands)

			LEVEL
71-02	PARADE of the TOY SOLDIERS	Jessel	1
71-07	HARK the HERALD ANGELS SING	Traditional	2

FOOD

55-38 •	HURRY, LITTLE PIZZA CAR	Holmes	1

HALLOWEEN

55-40 *•	GALLOPING GHOSTS (Minor Key)	Weston/Schaum	2
52-15 *•	SPOOK HOUSE (Left Hand Melody)	Schaum	1
52-20 *•	SPUNKY SPOOKS (Both Hands in Bass)	Weston	1

JAZZ STYLE

55-48 •	DUDE	Weston	2

LEFT HAND MELODY

52-22 •	KNOCKING AT MY DOOR ☝	Schaum	1
52-03 *•	LUMBERJACK SONG	Schaum	1
55-50 •	SCOTTISH SKETCH	Holmes	2

MARCHES

52-34 •	FANFARE	King	1
55-06	PARADE of the TOY SOLDIERS	Jessel	2

MINOR KEY

55-52 •	DREAM CATCHER	Holmes	2
52-28 •	SECRET AGENT	Weston	1

MOVIE THEME

80-01	STAR WARS (Main Title)	Williams	2

OLDIES but GOODIES

52-02 *	IN MY MERRY OLDSMOBILE	Edwards	1
52-21 ✓	SCHOOL DAYS	Edwards	1

RAGTIME

55-21 *✓	ENTERTAINER (Easy Version)	Joplin	2

SACRED

55-25 *✓	HOW GREAT THOU ART	Swedish Folk Melody	2

SPORTS

52-10 *•	CHEERLEADER	Plank	1
52-18 *•	JOGGING TRAIL ☝ (Minor Key)	Payne	1
55-43 •	ROLLER BLADES	Schaum	2
52-41 •	SKI TRAILS	King	1
55-28 ✓	TAKE ME OUT TO THE BALL GAME	Von Tilzer	2

SPRINGTIME

55-18 *•	FAWN'S LULLABY	Masson	2
52-04 *	SPRING, SWEET SPRING	Lincke	1
52-31 *•	TREES IN THE BREEZE	Hampton	1

STACCATO

55-23 *•	FRISKY FROG (Both Hands in Treble)	Cahn	2
52-33 •	HOPSCOTCH	Hampton	1
52-11 *•	WINDSHIELD WIPER ROCK (Staccato)	Noblitt	1

THANKSGIVING

52-24 *•	PERKY TURKEY	Weston	1
55-12	THANKSGIVING SCENE	Medley of 4 Hymns	2

WALTZES

52-30 •	OPUS ONE	Cahn	1